MODERN EUROPEAN VERSE

THE POCKET POETS

THE POCKET POETS
★

ALTAR AND PEW Selected by John Betjeman
BAUDELAIRE Translated by Roy Campbell
'BEAT' POETS Selected by Gene Baro
BURNS Love Songs
CHRISTINA ROSSETTI Selected by Naomi Lewis
COMIC VERSE Selected by David Herbert
COUNTRY POEMS Selected by Geoffrey Grigson
DANNIE ABSE
D. H. LAWRENCE Love Poems
EDITH SITWELL
EDWARD LEAR Nonsense Songs
EDWARD THOMAS
ELIZABETHAN LOVE LYRICS Selected by John Hadfield
FAMOUS AMERICAN POEMS Selected by Gene Baro
GEORGIAN POETS Selected by Alan Pryce-Jones
GERARD MANLEY HOPKINS
GEORGE HERBERT Selected by David Herbert
JAZZ POEMS Selected by Anselm Hollo
JOHN BETJEMAN
JOHN DONNE Love Poems
JOHN KEATS Selected by David Herbert
LAURIE LEE
LIVING VOICES Selected by Jon Silkin
LEWIS CARROLL Nonsense Verse
MODERN EUROPEAN VERSE Selected by Dannie Abse
MODERN RUSSIAN POETRY Translated by Jack Lindsay
NEGRO VERSE Selected by Anselm Hollo
NEW VOICES Selected by Alan Pryce-Jones
RICHARD CHURCH
ROCHESTER Selected by Robert Duncan
RUPERT BROOKE
SHAKESPEARE Songs from the Plays
TENNYSON Selected by Raymond Mortimer
WALTER DE LA MARE Selected by John Hadfield

THE POCKET POETS

MODERN EUROPEAN VERSE

Selected by
DANNIE ABSE

LONDON · VISTA BOOKS

FIRST PUBLISHED IN 1964 BY
VISTA BOOKS · LONDON

MADE AND PRINTED IN GREAT BRITAIN BY
THE GARDEN CITY PRESS LIMITED
LETCHWORTH, HERTFORDSHIRE

© VISTA BOOKS 1964

CONTENTS

BERTOLT BRECHT: *To Posterity*	9
Changing the Wheel	11
C. P. CAVAFY: *Expecting the Barbarians*	12
Candles	13
PAUL CELAN: *Death Fugue*	14
ZBIGNIEW HERBERT: *The Seventh Angel*	16
MIGUEL HERNANDEZ: *Hear This Voice*	18
JUAN RAMÓN JIMÉNEZ: *To the Sonnet with my Soul*	21
FEDERICO GARCÍA LORCA: *The Faithless Wife*	22
Somnambulistic Ballad	24
ITZIK MANGER: *Jealous Adam*	27
V. V. MAYAKOVSKY: *Suicide Note*	29
BORIS PASTERNAK: *First Frost*	30
No Title	31
It is not Seemly	32
JACQUES PRÉVERT: *Exercise Book*	33
How to Paint the Portrait of a Bird	35
SALVATORE QUASIMODO: *Thanatos Athanatos*	37
RAINER MARIA RILKE:	
Two Poems from *The Book of Hours*	38
Autumn	39
On the Sunny Road	40
The Boy	41
GEORGE SEFERIS: from *Mythical Story*	42
from *Gymnopaedia*	43
ANGHELOS SIKELIANOS: *Unwritten*	45
YEVGENY YEVTUSHENKO: *Babiy Yar*	47

INTRODUCTION

TWENTY-FIVE years ago, the work of European poets such as Rilke and Lorca was read in England with great avidity. Not only were poetry readers internationally minded but the English poets themselves seemed to be engaged emotionally and polemically with the political happenings in Europe. Such writers reacted unequivocally, like litmus paper to acid, to European conflict—to the civil war in Spain, for example. They were hostile in their writings, and in their ancillary activities, to the rise of Nazism in Germany and Fascism in Italy. But fashions change, so that not long after World War II had ended, if an English poet proclaimed in his work a similar, engaged interest in the social upheavals of distant countries he would, undoubtedly, have been labelled a political romantic—and, by then, the very word 'romantic', in critical parlance, had become almost a dirty word.

Indeed, by the 1950's, critical opinion in England had ventured to the opposite extreme, and the virtues in poetry, primarily praised, were those that could be singled out as distinctively English. Poets like Eliot and Pound whose influences and interest were obviously European in scope were downgraded, and Hardy, Edward Thomas, Robert Graves, achieved a new popularity. Though poets such as Edward Thomas have their own attraction and excellence, many looking back may, nevertheless, come to think that much ephemeral reviewing and criticism in England during this period was marked and limited by a barely conscious chauvinism. In any event, a criticism which countenanced poetry as a kind of genteel, social accomplishment could hardly spotlight favourably the vigorous, and rather differently ordered poetry that was being written abroad.

There are signs, though, that such a parochial critical climate is coming to an end, and this trend is reflected not least in the new revived interest in European poetry generally. Recently, there have been numerous anthologies of translations published, including one of 20th century Polish poetry, another of 20th century Yugoslavian poetry, and yet another of 20th century German poetry, and so on. There have been several public readings of European poetry in translation which have been well attended and kindly received. A book like Robert Lowell's *Imitations* too, with his free versions of European poems has been welcomed and abundantly praised. Poets, critics, and editors, then, are once again encouraging readers to develop more eclectic tastes and so the work of modern European poets is being explored.

Not infrequently, such European poets have been committed to more than their poetry. Unlike English poets they have not, after all, been living necessarily in a mild, fortunate, and liberal political ambience. Many have been subjected to grim social pressures which, by and large, English poets have happily escaped. Amongst the contributors to this anthology one has only to think of Lorca murdered, Mayakovsky committing suicide, Hernandez dying in a Franco prison, Celan surviving a Nazi concentration camp, Brecht exiled, and so on. It is not surprising therefore, that from Europe we have had much 'platform' poetry—poetry that is missionary, poetry that was not written to delight the reader but to arouse his indignation and, perhaps, move him to action. In the first world war our own Wilfred Owen confessed to a similar intention.

However, many celebrated poems from Hungary, Poland, etc.—e.g. Gyula Illyes' 'One Sentence on Tyranny,' or Adam Wazyk's 'Poem for Adults,' have not been included in this anthology for, in the opinion of this editor, such work is of more interest to the sociologist and political historian than to the poetry reader. Indeed, though there are several samples of aesthetically satisfying 'platform' poetry to be found here—for example Hernandez's moving 'Hear This Voice' which was written during the Spanish civil war—many inclusions are interiorly composed and directed, and not written at the top of their voices. There are exclusions, too, of poems by European poets most eminent, among them Valéry and Montale, but this is either because of length, or because the English versions, in my view, are not faithful enough or, if faithful, not satisfactory enough as poetry. There is, I hope, nothing to apologise for in this anthology—only for what, because of such reasons, had to be regretfully left out.

DANNIE ABSE

ACKNOWLEDGMENTS

For permission to reprint copyright matter, the following acknowledgments are made: for 'To Posterity' (from Volume 4 of *Gedichte*) and 'Changing the Wheel', both by Bertolt Brecht, to the Brecht Estate, Suhrkamp Verlag (German publishers of *Gedichte*) and Messrs Methuen (English publishers of *Tales from the Calendar*); for two poems by C. P. Cavafy, to the author and The Hogarth Press; for a poem by Paul Celan, to the author, Deutsche Verlags-Anstalt and 'Commentary', New York; for a poem by Zbigniew Herbert, to the author and Mr Z. Najder; for a poem by Miguel Hernandez and for 'The Faithless Wife' by Federico García Lorca, to Mr Stephen Spender; for a poem by Juan Ramón Jiménez, to the author's executors; for 'Somnambulistic Ballad', to Messrs Bowes & Bowes; for a poem by Itzik Manger from 'Caravan' to Thomas Yoseloff; for a poem by V. V. Mayakovsky, to Mr Erik Korn and 'Poetry and Poverty', London; for 'It is not Seemly', from *Poems by B. Pasternak*, to Mr Peter Russell; for two other poems by Boris Pasternak, to Messrs Wm. Collins and The Harvill Press; for two poems by Jacques Prévert, from Paul Dehn's *Romantic Landscape*, to Messrs Hamish Hamilton; for a poem by Salvatore Quasimodo, to the author; for two poems from *The Book of Hours* by Rainer Maria Rilke, to Vision Press Ltd; for three poems from the *Selected Works* of Rainer Maria Rilke, to The Hogarth Press; for a passage from 'Mythical Story' by George Seferis and for a poem by Anghelos Sikelianos, both from *Six Poets of Modern Greece*, to Messrs Thames & Hudson; for a passage from 'Gymnopaedia' by George Seferis, to The Bodley Head; and for a poem by Yevgeny Yevtushenko from *Yevtushenko: Selected Poems* to Penguin Books.

BERTOLT BRECHT

TO POSTERITY

I

TRULY, the age I live in is bleak.
The guileless word is foolish. A smooth brow
Denotes insensitiveness. The laughing man
Has only not yet received
The dreadful news.

What times are these when a conversation
About trees is almost a crime.
Because it includes a silence about so many misdeeds!
That one there calmly crossing the street,
Hasn't he ceased to be at home to
His friends in need?

True enough: I still earn my living.
But, believe me, it's only luck.
Nothing I do gives me the right to eat my fill.
It happens that I've been spared. (When my luck gives out
I shall be lost.)

They tell me: Eat and drink. Be glad that you can!
But how can I eat and drink, when
From the hungry man I snatch what I eat, and
My glass of water deprives the man dying of thirst?
And yet I eat and drink.

And I'd also like to be wise.
In the old books you read what is wise:
To keep out of the strife of the world and spend
Your brief span without fear.

And to refrain from violence
Render good for evil
Not fulfil one's desires, but forget
Is accounted wise.
All these are beyond me:
Truly, the age I live in is bleak.

II

I came into the cities at the time of disorder
When hunger was rife.
I mixed with men at the time of rebellion
And revolted as they did.
So passed the time
Granted to me on earth.

I ate my meals between battles.
I lay down to sleep between the murderers.
Love I pursued unheeding
And on nature looked without patience.
So passed the time
Granted to me on earth.

The streets led into morasses in my time.
Speech betrayed me to the butcher.
There was little I could do. Yet the rulers
Sat more secure but for me, that was my hope.
So passed the time
Granted to me on earth.

My resources were not great. The goal
Lay far ahead.
It was clearly visible, if for me
Scarcely attainable.
So passed the time
Granted to me on earth.

III

You that will emerge from the deluge
In which we drowned,
When you speak of our shortcomings
Remember too
The bleak age
Which you have escaped.

For, changing countries more often than shoes, we walked
Through the wars of the classes, despairing
When there was injustice only and no rebellion.

And yet we know well:
Even hatred of vileness
Distorts a man's features.
Even anger at injustice
Makes hoarse his voice. Ah, we
Who desired to prepare the soil for kindness
Could not ourselves be kind.

But you, when the times permit
Men to be the helpers of men
Remember us
With indulgence.

Translated from the German by Michael Hamburger

CHANGING THE WHEEL

I sit on the roadside bank.
The driver changes a wheel.
I do not like the place I have come from.
I do not like the place I am going to.
Why do I watch him changing the wheel
With impatience?

Translated from the German by Michael Hamburger

C. P. CAVAFY

EXPECTING THE BARBARIANS

WHAT are we waiting for, assembled in the public square?

The barbarians are to arrive today.

Why such inaction in the Senate?
Why do the Senators sit and pass no laws?

Because the barbarians are to arrive today.
What further laws can the Senators pass?
When the barbarians come they will make the laws.

Why did our emperor wake up so early,
and sit at the principal gate of the city,
on the throne, in state, wearing his crown?

Because the barbarians are to arrive today.
And the emperor waits to receive
their chief. Indeed he has prepared
to give him a scroll. Therein he engraved
many titles and names of honour.

Why have our two consuls and the praetors come out
today in their embroidered togas;
why do they wear amethyst-studded bracelets,
and rings with brilliant glittering emeralds;
why are they carrying costly canes today,
superbly carved with silver and gold?

Because the barbarians are to arrive today,
and such things dazzle the barbarians.

Why don't the worthy orators come as usual
to make their speeches, to have their say?

Because the barbarians are to arrive today;
and they get bored with eloquence and orations.

Why this sudden unrest and confusion?
(How solemn their faces have become.)
Why are the streets and squares clearing quickly,
and all return to their homes, so deep in thought?

Because night is here but the barbarians have not come.
Some people arrived from the frontiers,
and they said that there are no longer any barbarians.

And now what shall become of us without any barbarians?
Those people were a kind of solution.

Translated from the Greek by Rae Dalven

CANDLES

THE days of our future stand before us
like a row of little lighted candles—
golden, warm, and lively little candles.

The days gone by remain behind us,
a mournful line of burnt-out candles;
the nearest ones are still smoking,
cold candles, melted and bent.

I do not want to look at them; their form saddens me,
and it saddens me to recall their first light.
I look ahead at my lighted candles.

I do not want to turn back, lest I see and shudder—
how quickly the sombre line lengthens,
how quickly the burnt-out candles multiply.

Translated from the Greek by Rae Dalven

PAUL CELAN

DEATH FUGUE

BLACK milk of the dawn we drink it evenings
we drink it noon and morning we drink it nights
we drink and drink
we dig a grave in the wind you won't lie cramped there
A man lives in the house who plays with the snakes who writes
who writes at dusk to Germany your golden hair Margarete
he writes it and comes out of the house and the stars twinkle he whistles his hounds out
he whistles forth his Jews has a grave dug in the ground
he orders us strike up now for the dance

Black milk of the dawn we drink you nights
we drink you morning and noon we drink you evenings
we drink and drink
A man lives in the house who plays with the snakes who writes
who writes at dusk to Germany your golden hair Margarete
Your ashen hair Sulamith we dig a grave in the wind you won't lie cramped there

He cries dig deeper in the ground you ones you others sing and play
he reaches for the iron in his belt he swings it his eyes are blue
dig your spades deeper you ones you others keep playing for the dance

Black milk of the dawn we drink you nights
we drink you noon and morning we drink you evenings

we drink and drink
a man lives in the house your golden hair Margarete
your ashen hair Sulamith he plays with the snakes

He cries play death sweeter death is a master from Germany
he cries fiddle lower then you'll rise in the air as smoke
then you'll have a grave in the clouds you won't lie cramped there

Black milk of the dawn we drink you nights
we drink you noon death is a master from Germany
we drink you evenings and mornings we drink and drink
death is a master from Germany his eye is blue
he strikes you with leaden balls his aim is true
a man lives in the house your golden hair Margarete
he sicks his hounds on us he gives us the gift of a grave in the air
he plays with the snakes death is a master from Germany
your golden hair Margarete
your ashen hair Sulamith

Translated from the German by Clement Greenberg

ZBIGNIEW HERBERT

THE SEVENTH ANGEL

The seventh angel
is completely different
even his name is different
Szemkel

he is not like Gabriel
the golden
pillar of the throne
and baldachin

nor like Raphael
the choir-tuner

nor even
Azrael
engineer of the planets
geometer of infinity
splendid exponent of theoretical physics

Szemkel
is black and nervous
and has been fined many times for
illegal import of sinners

between the abyss
and the heavens
without a rest his feet go pit-a-pit

his sense of dignity is non-existent
and they only keep him in the squad
out of consideration for the number seven

but he is not like the others
not like the hetman of the hosts
Michael
all scales and feathery plumes

nor like Azrafael
interior decorator of the universe
warden of its luxuriant vegetation
his wings shimmering like two oak trees

nor even like
Dedrael
apologist and cabalist

Szemkel Szemkel
. . . the angels complain
why can't you be splendid?

the Byzantine artists
when they paint all seven
reproduce Szemkel
just like the rest

because they fear
they might lapse into heresy
if they were to portray him
just as he is
black nervous
with his old halo tarnished.

Translated from the Polish by Peter Dale Scott

MIGUEL HERNANDEZ

HEAR THIS VOICE

Nations of the earth, fatherlands of the sea, brothers
of the world and of nothing:
inhabitants lost and more distant
from the sight than from the heart,
here I have a voice impassioned,
here I have a life challenged and indignant,
here I have a message, here I have a life.

Look, I am opened, like a wound.
Look, I am drowned, drowned
in the midst of my people and its ills.
Wounded I go, wounded and badly wounded,
bleeding through the trenches and hospitals.

Men, worlds, nations,
pay heed, listen to my cry pouring out blood,
gather together the pulses of my breaking heart
into your spacious hearts,
because I clutch the soul when I sing.

Singing I defend myself
and I defend my people when the barbarians of crime
imprint on my people their hooves
of powder and desolation.

This is their work, this:
passing, they destroy like the whirlwind,
and before their funereal choler
the horizons are arms and the roads are death.

The lament pouring through valleys and balconies,
deluges the stones and works in the stones,
and there is no room for so much death
and there is no wood for so many coffins.

Caravans of beaten-down bodies.
All is bandages, pain and handkerchiefs
all is stretchers on which the wounded
have broken their strength and their wings.

Blood, blood through the trees and the soil,
blood in the waters and on the walls,
and a fear that Spain will collapse
from the weight of the blood which soaks through her meshes
right to the bread which is eaten.

Gather together this gale,
nations, men, worlds,
which proceeds from the mouths of impassioned breath
and from hospitals of the dying.

Apply your ears
to my clamour of a violated people,
to the 'ay' of so many mothers, to the groans
of many a lucid being whom grief devoured.

The breasts which drove and wounded the mountains
see them languish without milk or beauty,
and see the white sweethearts and the black eyelashes
fallen and submissive in an obscure siesta.

Apply the passion of your entrails
to this people which dies with an invincible gesture

scattered by the lips and the brow,
beneath the implacable aeroplanes
which snatch terribly,
terribly ignominiously, every day,
sons from the hands of their mothers.

Cities of work and innocence,
youths who blossom from the oak,
trunks of bronze, bodies of potency,
lie precipitated into ruin.

A future of dust advances,
a fate advances
in which nothing will remain:
nor stone on stone nor bone on bone.

Spain is not Spain, it is an immense trench,
a vast cemetery red and bombarded:
the barbarians have willed it thus.

The earth will be a dense heart, desolated,
if you, nations, men, worlds,
with the whole of my people,
and yours as well on their side,
do not break the ferocious fangs.

Translated from the Spanish by Inez and Stephen Spender

JUAN RAMÓN JIMÉNEZ

TO THE SONNET WITH MY SOUL

As in the wing there is the infinite flight
which in the flower is the erring essence,
as in the flame there is the wandering
brilliance, and in the blue the single sky;

as the consolation in the melody,
the penetrating coolness in the stream,
the noble opulence in the diamond,
so in my flesh is the total desire.

In you, sonnet, form, this pristine hunger
imitates as in a lingering water
the multitude of its immortal wonders.

The endless clarity of your beauty is,
as the sky in a fountain, limitless
within the limitation of your borders.

Translated from the Spanish by W. S. Merwin

FEDERICO GARCÍA LORCA

THE FAITHLESS WIFE

So I took her to the river
believing she was a maiden,
but she already had a husband.

It was on Saint James's night
and almost as if I was obliged to.
The lanterns went out
and the crickets lighted up.
In the farthest street corners
I touched her sleeping breasts,
and they opened to me suddenly
like spikes of hyacinth.
The starch of her petticoat
sounded in my ears
like a piece of silk
rent by ten knives.
Without silver light on their foliage
the trees had grown larger
and a horizon of dogs
barked very far from the river.

Past the blackberries,
the reeds and the hawthorn,
underneath her cluster of hair
I made a hollow in the earth.
I took off my tie.
She took off her dress.
I my belt with the revolver.
She her four bodices.
Nor nard nor mother-o'-pearl

have skin so fine,
nor did crystals lit by moon
shine with such brilliance.
Her thighs slipped away from me
like startled fish,
half full of fire,
half full of cold.
That night I ran
on the best of roads
mounted on a nacre mare
without bridle or stirrups.
As a man, I won't repeat
the things she said to me.
The light of understanding
has made me most discreet.
Smeared with sand and kisses
I took her away from the river.
The swords of the lilies
battled with the air.

I behaved just like myself.
Like a proper gipsy.
I gave her a large sewing basket,
of straw-coloured satin,
and I did not fall in love
for although she had a husband
she told me she was a maiden
when I took her to the river.

*Translated from the Spanish by J. L. Gili
and Stephen Spender*

Federico García Lorca

SOMNAMBULISTIC BALLAD

Green, green, I want you green,
Green the wind and green the boughs,
The ship upon the ocean seen.
The horses on the hills that browse.
With the shadows round her waist
Upon her balcony she dreams.
Green her flesh and green her tresses.
In her eyes chill silver gleams.
Green, green, I want you green
While the gypsy moon beam plays,
Things at her are gazing keenly
But she cannot meet their gaze.

Green, green, I want you green.
See the great stars of the frost
Come rustling with the fish of shadow
To find the way the dawn has lost.
The figtree chafes the passing wind
With the sandpaper of its leaves,
And hissing like a thievish cat,
With bristled fur, the mountain heaves.
But who will come? And by what path?
On her verandah lingers she,
Green her flesh and green her hair,
Dreaming of the bitter sea.

'Companion, I should like to trade
My pony for your house and grange,
To swap my saddle for your mirror,
My sheath-knife for your rug to change.

Companion, I have galloped bleeding
From Cabra's passes down the range.'
  'If it could be arranged, my lad,
I'd clinch the bargain; but you see
Now I am no longer I,
Nor does my house belong to me.'
  'Companion, I should like to die
Respectably at home in bed,
A bed of steel if possible,
With sheets of linen smoothly spread.
Can you not see this gash I carry
From rib to throat, from chin to chest?'
  'Three hundred roses darkly red
Spatter the white front of your vest.
Your blood comes oozing out to spread,
Around your sash, its ghostly smell.
But now I am no longer I
Nor is my house my own to sell.'

Let me go up tonight at least,
And climb the dim verandah's height.
Let me go up! Oh let me climb
To the verandah green with light,
Oh chill verandahs of the moon
Whence fall the waters of the night!

And now the two companions climb
Up where the high verandah sheers,
Leaving a little track of blood,
Leaving a little trail of tears.
Trembling along the roofs, a thousand
Sparkles of tin reflect the ray.
A thousand tambourines of glass
Wounded the dawning of the day.

[25]

Green, green, I want you green.
Green the wind: and green the bough.
The two companions clambered up
And a long wind began to sough
Which left upon the mouth a savour
Of gall and mint and basil-flowers.
Companion! Tell me. Where is she?
Where is that better girl of ours?
How many times she waited for you!
How long she waited, hoped, and sighed,
Fresh her face, and black her tresses,
Upon this green verandah-side!

Over the surface of the pond
The body of the gypsy sways.
Green her flesh and green her tresses
Her eyes a frosty silver glaze.
An icicle hung from the moon—
Suspends her from the water there.
The night became as intimate
As if it were the village square.
The drunkards of the Civil Guard,
Banging the door, began to swear.
Green, oh green, I want you green.
Green the wind: and green the boughs
The ship upon the waters seen
The horses on the hill that browse.

Translated from the Spanish by Roy and Mary Campbell

ITZIK MANGER

JEALOUS ADAM

A yellow canary trilled
on a tree in paradise.
Between a song and a dream
Adam opened his eyes.

A red-hot sunray darted
across the dewy grass.
And chasing it were a weasel
and a rabbit running fast.

Adam smiled contented,
as he watched his beautiful Eve.
Her body as young as the day,
beneath a covering leaf.

He looked at her and thought,
enjoying the lovely sight:
Daylight is good by day,
as is the dark at night.

Then Adam rose and went
into the clamour of spring,
and in his breast he felt
the beat of every wing.

But listen! Down there in the valley
a river rushed ahead—
a little river—yet Adam,
he suddenly grew sad.

For in the water he saw
another Adam one day.
What is the Water-Adam up to,
and who is he anyway?

Perhaps it's true, perhaps it's not,
but how is one to know?
Maybe it's Adam—the other one—
who's playing with Eve just now.

He must go back at once,
and back in haste he went.
But there stood Eve and held
a cuckoo in her hand.

Tell me, she asked the bird,
whether I am really fair,
whether he truly loves me,
my husband, Adam dear?

And Adam, as he heard her voice,
did not know why it was,
he felt like burying his head
and sobbing in the grass.

Translated from the Yiddish by Jacob Sonntag

V. V. MAYAKOVSKY

(*Before he committed suicide Mayakovsky left this note*)

She loves me . . . she loves me not.
I tear my hands, scatter the broken fingers . . . loves me not.
As we scatter the random riddling heads of daisies
Tumbling through summer.

Though I adopt the smooth chin and greying hair,
The silver, tinkling out the change of years,
I hope, I know that age will never bring
The final shame of prudent commonsense.

It's after one and you must be asleep.
The milky way is like a silver river.
I'm in no hurry. There's no need
To wake you or disturb you with telegrams or thunder.

It's what they call the end of the affair.
Love's gondola has struck the rocks of fact.
We're quits—no point in totting up
Our score of troubles, miseries, and wrongs.

See how much peace the world can give.
The sky is wrapped in stars, the gift of night.
At such a time you rise, and find you speak
To all the years, the future, and the world.

It's after one and you must be asleep.
Or maybe you can feel the night as well.
I'm in no hurry. There's no need
To wake you or disturb you with telegrams or thunder.

Translated from the Russian by Erik Korn

BORIS PASTERNAK

FIRST FROST

Pillar of fire in smoke, the sun
   In the haze of a frosty morning
      Sees me as blurred
      As a bad photo;

Blazes a trail through pond and meadow
   Enabling puzzled trees
      To pick me out
      Across the water.

Identified too late, a body
   Drowns in the mist. The frost
      Has goose-flesh, smarmy
      With air like rouge.

Sacking of hoarfrost wads the paths.
   The earth is sick and tired
      Of cold and the stink
      Of potato stalks.

Translated from the Russian by Michael Harari

Boris Pasternak

NO TITLE

Miss touch-me-not's on fire,
The prude of every day.
In the dark turret of a poem
I'll lock your looks away.

The lampshade's fiery skin
Transforms the room, makes free
With cramped walls, window sill,
Our shadows, you and me.

You tuck your feet beneath you
Like a Turk, on the divan,
Reason (you always do)
As only children can,

Daydream, threading the beads
That spilt across your dress,
Look much too sad and chatter
With too much artlessness.

You're right, I must rename love;
It's a word we have all worn through.
If you like, I'll christen the world
And all its words, for you.

But how can dark looks show me
What ore of feeling lies
At the hidden mine of your heart?
Why do you cloud your eyes?

Translated from the Russian by Michael Harari

Boris Pasternak

IT IS NOT SEEMLY

It is not seemly to be famous,
Celebrity does not exalt;
There is no need to hoard your writings
And to preserve them in a vault.

To give your all—this is creation,
And not—to deafen and eclipse.
How shameful, when you have no meaning,
To be on everybody's lips!

Try not to live as a pretender,
But so to manage your affairs
That you are loved by wide expanses
And hear the call of future years.

Leave blanks in life—not in your papers,
And do not ever hesitate
To pencil out whole chunks, whole chapters
Of your existence, of your fate.

Into obscurity retiring,
Your progress in it try to hide,
As disappears on early mornings
In autumn mist the countryside.

Another, step by step, will follow
The living imprint of your feet;
But you yourself must not distinguish
Your victory from your defeat.

And never for a single moment
Betray your *credo* or pretend.
But be alive—this only matters—
Alive and burning to the end.

Translated from the Russian by Lydia Pasternak Slater

JACQUES PRÉVERT

EXERCISE BOOK

Two and two four
four and four eight
eight and eight sixteen . . .
Once again! says the master
Two and two four
four and four eight
eight and eight sixteen.
But look! the lyre-bird
high on the wing
the child sees it
the child hears it
the child calls it
Save me
play with me
bird!
So the bird alights
and plays with the child
Two and two four
Once again! says the master
and the child plays
and the bird plays too . . .
Four and four eight
eight and eight sixteen
and twice sixteen makes what?
Twice sixteen makes nothing
least of all thirty-two
anyhow
and off they go.
For the child has hidden
the bird in his desk

and all the children
hear its song
and all the children
hear the music
and eight and eight in their turn
off they go
and four and four and two and two
in their turn fade away
and one and one make neither one nor two
but one by one off they go.
And the lyre-bird sings
and the child sings
and the master shouts
When you've quite finished playing the fool!
But all the children
are listening to the music
and the walls of the classroom
quietly crumble.
The windowpanes turn
once more to sand
the ink is sea
the desk is trees
the chalk is cliffs
and the quill pen
a bird again.

Translated from the French by Paul Dehn

Jacques Prévert

HOW TO PAINT THE PORTRAIT OF A BIRD

First paint a cage
with an open door
then paint
something pretty
something simple
something fine
something useful
for the bird
next place the canvas against a tree
in a garden
in a wood
or in a forest
hide behind the tree
without speaking
without moving . . .
Sometimes the bird comes quickly
but it can also take many years
before making up its mind
Don't be discouraged
wait
wait if necessary for years
the quickness or the slowness of the coming
of the bird having no relation
to the success of the picture
When the bird comes
if it comes
observe the deepest silence
wait for the bird to enter the cage
and when it has entered
gently close the door with the paint-brush
then

one by one paint out all the bars
taking care not to touch one feather of the bird
Next make a portrait of the tree
choosing the finest of its branches
for the bird
paint also the green leaves and the freshness of the wind
dust in the sun
and the sound of the grazing cattle in the heat of summer
and wait for the bird to decide to sing
If the bird does not sing
it is a bad sign
a sign that the picture is bad
but if it sings it is a good sign
a sign that you are ready to sign
so then you pluck very gently
one of the quills of the bird
and you write your name in a corner of the picture.

Translated from the French by Paul Dehn

SALVATORE QUASIMODO

THANATOS ATHANATOS

And shall we have to deny thee then,
God of the tumours, God of the living
flower, begin with a no to the obscure
rock 'I am,' consent to death
and on each tomb inscribe our only
certainty: 'thanatos athanatos'?
Without a name to tell the dreams
the tears the furors of this man
defeated by still-open questions.
Our dialogue alters; now the absurd
becomes possible. There, beyond
the smoke of fog, within the trees
the potency of leaves awakes,
true is the river pressing on the banks.
Life is not dream. True is man
and his jealous plaint of silence.
God of silence, open solitude.

Translated from the Italian by Allen Mandelbaum

RAINER MARIA RILKE

Two poems from THE BOOK OF HOURS

I

If only there were stillness, full, complete.
If all the random and approximate
were muted, with neighbours' laughter, for your sake,
and if the clamour that my senses make
did not confound the vigil I would keep—

Then in a thousandfold thought I could think
you out, even to your utmost brink,
and (while a smile endures) possess you, giving
you away, as though I were but giving thanks,
to all the living.

II

Put out my eyes, and I can see you still;
slam my ears to, and I can hear you yet;
and without any feet can go to you;
and tongueless, I can conjure you at will.
Break off my arms, I shall take hold of you
and grasp you with my heart as with a hand;
arrest my heart, my brain will beat as true;
and if you set this brain of mine afire,
then on my blood-stream I yet will carry you.

Translated from the German by Babette Deutsch

Rainer Maria Rilke

AUTUMN

The leaves are falling, falling as from far,
as though above were withering farthest gardens;
they fall with a denying attitude.

And night by night, down into solitude,
the heavy earth falls far from every star.

We are all falling. This hand's falling too—
all have this falling-sickness none withstands.

And yet there's always One whose gentle hands
this universal falling can't fall through.

Translated from the German by J. B. Leishman

Rainer Maria Rilke

ON THE SUNNY ROAD

On the sunny road, within the hollow
cloven tree, that now for generations
has been a trough, inaudibly renewing
a little film of water, I can still my
thirst by letting all that pristine freshness
ripple from my wrists through all my body.
Drinking seems to me too much, too open:
this more patient, more expectant gesture
fills my consciousness with sparkling water.

If you came, then, I could be contented
just to let my hands rest very lightly
either on your shoulders' youthful rounding
or upon your breasts' responsive pressure.

Translated from the German by J. B. Leishman

Rainer Maria Rilke

THE BOY

I'D like, above all, to be one of those
who drive with wild black horses through the night,
torches like hair uplifted in affright
when the great wind of their wild hunting blows.
I'd like to stand in front as in a boat,
tall, like a long floating flag unrolled.
And dark, but with a helmet made of gold,
restlessly flashing. And behind to ride
ten other looming figures side by side,
with helmets all unstable like my own,
now clear like glass, now old and blank like stone.
And one to stand by me and blow us space
with the brass trumpet that can blaze and blare,
blowing a black solitude through which we tear
like dreams that speed too fast to leave a trace.
Houses behind us fall upon their knees,
alleys cringe crookedly before our train,
squares break in flight: we summon and we seize:
we ride, and our great horses rush like rain.

Translated from the German by J. B. Leishman

GEORGE SEFERIS

from MYTHICAL STORY

3

'REMEMBER the bath by which you were slain' Aeschylus.

I awoke with this marble head in my hands
which exhausts my elbows and I do not know where to set
    it down.
It was falling into the dream as I was coming out of the
    dream
so our lives joined and it will be very difficult to part them.

I look at the eyes: neither open nor closed
I speak to the mouth which keeps trying to speak
I hold the cheeks which have passed beyond the skin
I have no more strength.

My hands disappear and come back to me
mutilated.

*Translated from the Greek by Edmund Keeley
and Philip Sherrard*

George Seferis

from GYMNOPAEDIA (II. MYCENAE)

Give me your hands, give me your hands, give me your
 hands
I saw in the night
The mountain's pointed peak
I saw the plain afar flooded in moonlight
And no moon to be seen;
I saw, turning my head,
Black stones huddled around
And all my life stretched out like a string,
The beginning and the ending,
The final moment
My hands.

Needs must he sink who carries the great stones;
These stones I have carried as long as I was able,
These stones I have loved as long as I was able,
These stones my fate.
Wounded by my own soil
Tortured by my own garment
Condemned by my own gods,
These stones.

I know they do not know; yet I
Who have so often followed
The path that leads from murderer to victim
From victim to punishment
And from the punishment up to another murder;
Groping my way
Over the purple welling inexhaustible
That night of the return

When the whistling began
Of Furies in the scanty grass—
I have seen snakes crossed with vipers
Knotted about the accursed generation
Our fate.

Voices out of stone, out of sleep,
Voices more deep here where the world grows dark,
Memory of toil that is rooted in the rhythm
Beaten upon the earth by feet forgotten.
Bodies sunk, all naked, in the foundations
Of the other time. Eyes
Staring and staring towards a sign
That you, however you wish it, cannot distinguish.
The soul
That fights to become your soul.

Even the silence is no longer yours
Here where the mill stones have stopped still.

Translated from the Greek by **Rex Warner**

ANGHELOS SIKELIANOS

UNWRITTEN

A LITTLE while before the sun had set,
as Jesus and his disciples were out walking
beyond the walls of Zion, they unexpectedly
came near the quarter where for years the town
had dumped its refuse—burnt mattresses
of the sick, broken crocks, rags, rubbish, filth.

And there, upon the highest mound, its legs
turned skyward, lay a dog's bloated carcass
which, as the crows covering it took flight
when suddenly they heard the footsteps, gave out
such stench that all the disciples, holding
their breath with their hands, as one man drew back.

But Jesus, walking calmly on alone
towards the mound, stopped short and gazed upon
the carcass so, that one of the disciples,
not able to restrain himself, cried out
to him from afar: 'Master, do you not sense
the terrible smell, that you stand there in that way?'

And he, his eyes not moving from the spot
at which he gazed, replied: 'He with pure breath
will even in the town from which we come
breathe the terrible stench . . . But now I marvel
with all my soul at what from this decay
there issues . . . See how that dog's teeth are sparkling
in the sun; like hailstone, like the lily,
beyond the putrefaction, a great promise,
reflection of the Eternal, but still more

the harsh hope and lightning-flash of Justice!'
Thus He spoke; and whether the disciples
understood these words or not, together,
as He moved on, they followed once again
His silent path . . .

   And now, how I, indeed
the least of men, do turn my mind, O Lord,
toward Your words, and on one thought intent
before You stand: Ah! grant, grant to me even
as I now walk outside the town of Zion,
and from the earth's one end until the other
all is desolation, all is rubbish,
all unburied corpses which choke up
the sacred spring of breath, within the city
or outside the city; grant, O Lord, to me
amid this frightful stench through which I pass
for one moment only Your holy calm,
so that I too, dispassionate, may pause
among this carrion and somewhere seize
with my own eyes a token, white as hailstone,
as the lily, something sparkling suddenly
deep within me, outside the putrefaction,
beyond the world's decay, like the dog's teeth
at which that evening as You gazed upon them
You, O Lord, had marvelled, a great promise,
reflection of the Eternal, but still more
the harsh hope and lightning-flash of Justice! . . .

Translated from the Greek by Edmund Keeley
and Philip Sherrard

YEVGENY YEVTUSHENKO

BABIY YAR

Over Babiy Yar
there are no memorials.
The steep hillside like a rough inscription.
I am frightened.
Today I am as old as the Jewish race.
I seem to myself a Jew at this moment.
I, wandering in Egypt.
I, crucified. I perishing.
Even today the mark of the nails.
I think also of Dreyfus. I am he.
The Philistine my judge and my accuser.
Cut off by bars and cornered,
ringed round, spat at, lied about;
the screaming ladies with the Brussels lace
poke me in the face with parasols.
I am also a boy in Belostok,
the dropping blood spreads across the floor,
the public-bar heroes are rioting
in an equal stench of garlic and of drink.
I have no strength, go spinning from a boot,
shriek useless prayers that they don't listen to;
with a cackle of 'Thrash the kikes and save Russia!'
the corn-chandler is beating up my mother.
I seem to myself like Anna Frank
to be transparent as an April twig
and am in love, I have no need for words,
I need for us to look at one another.
How little we have to see or to smell
separated from foliage and the sky,
how much, how much in the dark room
gently embracing each other.

They're coming. Don't be afraid.
The booming and banging of the spring.
It's coming this way. Come to me.
Quickly, give me your lips.
They're battering in the door. Roar of the ice.

Over Babiy Yar
rustle of the wild grass.
The trees look threatening, look like judges.
And everything is one silent cry.
Taking my hat off
I feel myself slowly going grey.
And I am one silent cry
over the many thousands of the buried;
am every old man killed here,
every child killed here.
O my Russian people, I know you.
Your nature is international.
Foul hands rattle your clean name.
I know the goodness of my country.
How horrible it is that pompous title
the anti-semites calmly call themselves,
Society of the Russian People.
No part of me can ever forget it.
When the last anti-semite on the earth
is buried for ever
let the International ring out.
No Jewish blood runs among my blood,
but I am as bitterly and hardly hated
by every anti-semite
as if I were a Jew. By this
I am a Russian.

*Translated from the Russian by Robin Milner-Gulland
and Peter Levi, S.J.*